Hiring Employees & Outsourcing

The Introduction

Let's start out with an introduction. Value of your time is every as bit important as is the question of experience and expertise you covet. I have opened and operated nearly two dozen medical clinics, built multiple furniture stores and consulted for mega million-dollar companies. I have been honored to partner with multimillionaires who owned over 20 Million in real estate, and trained businessmen and women all over the USA. I have made more mistakes than I want to admit, some that almost put us out of business, and others that helped make $500,000 weeks. I am a firm believer in understanding one's failure as well as one's success. This includes many industries, positions and age ranges. Great companies have secrets that others aren't aware are there. Social and financial goals are different in industries as are attitude towards working at a job or believing in a career. A great hire can make or break you company. Many companies believe hiring can be treated as a full-time position. Most businesses don't have the means to do this full time. For this reason, we need to get creative and be able to flatten the learning curve. This guide to hiring is an honest approach to do just that.

Let's star out by stating that I am aware that furniture stores, and medical clinic are totally different industries. My introduction may have you wondering how you get from one extreme to another. I started out working for a furniture wholesaler and as the business owner started to get in financial troubles, I was offered a way to buy the store I ran. This was my introduction to business ownership. I hit the ground running and never looked back. After opening my 3rd furniture store, I had a guy come in and talk to me about needing some furniture for a clinic his doctor was opening. After helping him with the furniture needs, he and I spoke about business. We had spent a couple days together and he was an intriguing guy to say the least. He asked me a question that I will never forget. What industry are you in? I said I am in the advertising industry. My product is furniture, but advertising is what make the business run. He looked at me smiled, and said you get it. What most people don't understand is that medical clinics are the same. It took me back… As the comparison from a furniture store to a medical clinic was never a thought I would consider. Until you start to look at one big similarity. Both industries require proper advertising to get clients on a large scale. Word of mouth is a start, but large-scale customer acquisition businesses need to get a lot more in dept to cover costs and payroll. I am not talking about hospitals, but small doctor run medical clinics. These types of clinics have three to five employees that are run by a physician or two. As with most businesses these industries have problems staffing and keeping quality staff. For a simple example: In Louisiana it is easy to keep a good medical assistant until they get approved to work on the oil rig. This will double their salary in many cases. How do you compete with these variables? You set the stage for success and ask the right questions from the get-go!

In addition to currently being an active member running three small medical clinics, I own and run a consulting company. My partner in this venture is Jessica Jones. Her background is in the advertising field. She has owned advertising companies for well over 20 years. This industry has lots of turnover in its own way. I have hired and trained in multiple industries, and many platforms, from Executive Officers, to VP's, Sales Managers and front desk employees. Every position is unique to the company and has turnover. In the case of top management, a lousy hire can potentially put a company out of business or destroy stock values. This is the responsibility you are taking on. Every hire is a choice that can both help and hurt a company. How you expect employees to dress can be a big problem or nothing at all.

I am writing this book as the Coronavirus in its early stage's March 2020. This is the 2nd in a how to guide I have written in my Business Series. I just made a downsizing decision due to this Coronavirus. Since I have some free time, I thought this would be a good time to help people with this very issue. I have been lucky enough to be mentored by many great businessmen and women. I take hiring and firing very seriously. When I offer a position to an employee, I am helping them with a position that may very well help feed his/her family. It is my duty and obligation to make the best hiring decision for the company. I believe we need to be sure about the decision. Creating a win-win is the ultimate reward. Down the road this can help a company take off or take the next step to become profitable. From the employee's standpoint, this can become a dream career with a company or institution of her choice. As with my first publication "Starting a Clinic in 4 Weeks" this is a step by step guide to help without having to read a 100-page book, and barely retaining anything. I want to give solid information so you a reference or review as needed. All my guides in this series will be short reads. I find many authors try to fill space. Both you and I have many things we want to accomplish. We need relevant information. Life is too short.

Let's start small. All business starts small with a few key members. Some companies have run for years with just a sole member like a dog grooming business. A dog groomer I have taken my dog to for 5 years has done a wonderful job running the business out of her garage. We will call her Lucy. Her business became so busy that she had to hire someone to keep up with demand. Lot's of businesses are in a similar situation. This can be scary; in this case I trusted her to take care of my Shih-tzu named Remy. He loved her and went potty on her floor every time I took him to get groomed. I believe this was a combination of nervous and excitement. Lucy told me that more than half of her dogs do this. I loved that she made me feel like it was normal. This was one of the small things she did to make me feel comfortable and build value. After the grooming, Remy was always happy as can be and would jump around with happiness. He would run circles around me and want to show off his new haircut. After years of doing everything herself Lucy brought on an employee part time. This was a smart and a well thought our move at this time. As another year went on Lucy decided to rent a space. The business has entered the critical stage where her garage was not enough. Over the 6 in business plus years she had acquired many tools to help her with efficiency, quality and to give her an edge with the competition.

After careful consideration she decided to get a small storefront the same area. When she was working out of her garage, there was nobody just walking in to check things out. Now in addition to having a 2nd part time groomer, she needed a front desk person or possibly a person that can do both. Now is when things get tricky. Lucy's current employee was just part time and could not take on a full-time position as she was still in school, so it's hiring time. With the addition of the storefront, not just a garage, and Lucy has more small additional duties to run the business than before. Lucy's store is currently grooming 7 and 15 dogs per day between her and the part time employee Martha. This brings in enough to pay her employee, rent, a little advertising, and most of the time a little for herself. As with most small businesses at this point Lucy had a hard time keeping her schedule consistent. On a day that she has 15 animals coming, there is not enough time in the day. Things are getting sloppy. Her fear was more about quality that quantity, but there must be a balance of both. For Lucy it was time to step back and analyze the situation. The storefront has more insurance needs, and small expenses.

We are at a fun and fearful position again. Lucy has a couple of extra small expenses she was not totally prepared for. To help offset this expense Lucy has just added a little bit more advertising to get a few more grooming sessions per day. This has created a scenario that her phone is getting a few more calls per day from advertising. The money she is spending on advertising is not cheap. Each call needs to be handled properly. Lucy knows how to answer the phone, but her dog groomer does not. Lucy decides to bring on that important 3rd person. Her current employee Martha is the daughter of a friend and had the same dog breed, so that hire was a no brainer. Martha loved animals as much as Lucy and wanted to become a Veterinarian. Martha just turned 17 years old and going off to college soon. Lucy was always aware that this day would come, and thought she'd be ready when it came.

Lucy decides to place a classified ad for a front desk person 20 hours per week. The scenario she was facing was 2-fold. The first is she needs to learn how to screen phone calls and applicants resumes. The 2nd is that she has advertisers calling from the ads she placed. There is barely enough time in the day to take care of everything. Lucy hires the first decent looking candidate that come in. She did her best to her ability with the 6 candidates that came in. Here new hire (we will call ger Angie) was a very energetic person. Lucy thought people would be drawn to her like they are Martha. Lucy knew that all issues were in her hands, as were rewards later when the business runs smooth. She did some phone training and showed Angie where all the supplies were. Angie already knew how to use the credit card processer. So far so good.

Being that this is her first real hiring decision, Lucy thinks she is moving in the right direction. Now she can go back to doing more grooming and taking care of each animal. Lucy covered the phone with Angie as previously discussed but did not make necessary precautions to be sure training was smooth. It is simple to assume people have the same passion we will have. Remember Martha was a seamless transition to the position she was hired for. Angie answered the phone for the first time, and a lady on the other end was mad that she could not get in that week. After the call Angie said she was not comfortable answering the phone as she does not like conflict. It was time to step back and try to understand the situation. After looking at the schedule Ms. Adams always came in the 3rd week of the month every 2 months. This was an unwritten rule and Angie was not aware of this. Angie said there was no room on the schedule. Lucy had just given her part time groomer Martha the day off as she was getting over-worked. Lucy realized quick that this was more than she could handle by herself. She needed to do more training with Angie or cross-train Martha. Every day by herself was a 10 to 12-hour day already. It was time to take a deep breath and look at the problems that she is facing. First, she called Ms. Adams back and took the blame for the mistake. As the person in charge of hiring, it is always your fault if the mistakes happened. Lucy realized there was many moving parts and it was not a small garage business anymore. There were more moving parts and not that much money to be spread around. Lucy needed some professional help.

Lucy called a few business colleagues and asked for advice. Everybody loved her and gave solid advice, but now she had many opinions and more to think about. Lucy found herself in a similar situation as many small businesses. She is more than aware that most small businesses need help in many areas. The problem is what advice do you use and not? The answer in most cases is right in front of you. Don't forget why you stated your business. The answer is usually in the place you forget. Your clients.

A few days later a solution presented itself when I brought Remy in. I noticed Lucy was stressed out and trying to fake her emotions. I asked her if there was anything I could do, she said not unless you can hire me a new person like today. Even though I have taken Remy to her for many years she did not know that I have been hiring for years and made years of mistakes. My first thought was my daughter. At just 11 years old I did not feel comfortable having her help. I asked Lucy how many contacts she had via email. She said she was not sure, but it was over easily over 100. Since I have worked with Lucy for years, I knew she was well liked. As she was grooming Remy, I let her know that there is power in her network of people and business colleagues. Later that night I wrote her an email describing her needs for a front desk person, and we sent to her current clients. She was amazed that people want to help her. I explained to her that she has earned this respect. There was a reason client were with her for many years. Three days later she had 2 excellent options from people that loved Lucy and her ability to take care of their pets. The lesson here is that you may have a great option in your network. Start there. Don't forget about people you have worked with or wanted to previously. There will be times when the task you are taking on seems impossible. No two businesses are the same when it come to hiring and firing, people that like you is always a good start.

Understanding Your Options

Your network can be the goldmine for many resources. This guide is specifically about staffing but understanding that your network has the same concerns allows you to get solid advice from other professionals. Most of her clients were businesspeople, more experienced or even have retired after working for 40 years. The amount of knowledge her clients have is fully untapped as of now. This consists people who have worked with you. This could include clients, patients, or people in Social Media, like LinkedIn and Facebook. Often you will find that these people will go above and beyond to get you help. Trust is not something that is earned in an advertisement or post online. When you tell a business colleague that you need a staff member, they are happy to help as this can come full circle later. Any person that is sent to will be filled in on everything you gave this person for qualifications. The odds of this person being qualified is much higher, as your network member will not want to just send you someone and looks silly in the process. They are putting their reputation on the line. If a person willing to commit at this level already, there is a solid chance of success.

Every time we fail at something, we are in the learning process. With every success we have we will be in the earning process. As you make hiring decisions look at all decisions this way. Evaluate the situation on how critical the position is to overall success. At first glance getting a person to sit of front and answer a few phones seems like a very simple and low stress task. As we dig a little deeper, we find out that this person will be the first person a customer sees or talks to. Now as we are working on the business of acquiring new customers and overall professionalism, who should this person be? If it were me, I would want the business owner taking on these responsibilities at this stage. The business owner is the only one who learns and earns. Just as importantly, Lucy is the one person who makes decisions and gets pays herself last based upon success or failure. Lucy has the most to gain and lose with each new client. Take a step back and analyze the need. This is not a small decision. It can cause you more headaches than it is worth if done wrong. I have made this mistake at all levels if hiring dozens of times. Those were all learning lessons on my part. It is cheaper to learn from some body else's mistakes than doing it yourself. Everybody makes mistakes, but the less you can make, the better off and more efficient you get.

There is always the concept of paid vs free. Your network will be highest quality and free. In a rarity in life you as a businessperson or hiring manager will feel better about an already stressful process. In many cases you have someone above you. As the business owner you must be responsible for taxes and need to report to the Government. As a hiring manager you may have an officer or VP who oversees you. Either way, this can make this process easier and make you look good in the process. Part of the title of this book is to save you time and money. By understanding your network, this is the pay off. If this was a solution every time, then you would not ever need to advertise.

Remember above my business partner Jessica Jones. I can say that Jessica, and 2 other businessmen I have worked with have taught me almost everything I know in the media space. I had the privilege to help build a neighborhood magazine almost a decade ago. This gave me the understanding of what people wanted and problems that were common. It often seemed like there were just a few concerns that the neighborhood had, once we answered these issues we were welcomed with open arms. This magazine would feature a family in the neighborhood each month. We once made the biggest goof of all time and misspelled the last name of the family being featured. We had to go back to them with our tails between our legs. Since the family had it delivered already, I was given the duty to go say I am sorry. Oddly enough it was not as big of a deal as I thought. Since people bought advertisements in the magazine it just highlighted even more that she was a unique stylist. Go figure, it wasn't that bad.

So why do I bring this up as an example you may be asking? This magazine did a lot of things for the entire neighborhood. Like small free classifieds for dog walkers, daycare in the neighborhood and yes it can be used as a free way to get help. Now going back to Lucy and the pet grooming.

This could have been an excellent way to advertise for free. People in the neighborhood are always looking for good help in many areas. People in this very neighborhood already use Lucy, so this is a no brainer. In all reality you are really doing yourself a disservice by not being in there. Now let's look at the other angle. If I were a dog groomer and I needed more clients. What would be a way to get this done with the right clients. I am I next to a neighborhood that had a magazine as many nice neighborhoods do. I might as well put an ad in there. As a crazy bonus you can get testimonials from current customers in the neighborhood. Part of the reason you put your location where you did, is because you already had clients in said subdivision. Simple efficient and cost effective. This is a win-win-win and takes care of a low-cost solution.

Let's go in the direction of a classified ad in the newspaper. The people reading the newspaper may have 5 dog groomers between you and them. The print has a lot more competition, and costs more. While you are reaching many readers, often you are getting non-qualified customers. The subdivision we just spoke about has 600 homes and 6 already use your service. There may only be 150 animals, buy every person that gets their dog groomed is a potential customer. Remember we wanted to get from 7 to 15 per day consistently. We are trying to get 5 or more new clients daily. The odds of getting 5 new clients in a subdivision that drives by your place on many days is very high. They see your name, know who you are, and best of all you are dog walking distance away. You may get 10 new clients, taking care of 2 days that you are at or near your goal. This pays for new staff, possibly gets you new staff options and will surely create positive word of mouth. Ultimately getting more clients.

Do I think there is a place for newspaper? Absolutely, I want to create a few scenarios that help fit many businesses. Let's not look at a mattress store. I know this space well as I used to own them. Advertising in that same neighborhood could be beneficial, but people only buy a bed so many times. They may not need another bed for 3, 4 or 5 years. The Dog walking is 3, 4 or 5 times per year. Big difference. The mattress is about a few things comfort, price, quality and name brand in many cases. I would start first and foremost in the newspaper, because this is a much bigger market and people will drive for a deal. The cost per sale is higher, so the cost of advertising per sale is much more effective.

I would add a few medias in the furniture industry. The business lends itself running new specials all the time. Dog grooming is more stable once the customer is attained. To add credibility to my newspaper I may run a TV spot. In this industry is about being in the right media. Presidents day, 4th of July, Valentines Day, Thanksgiving and other holiday sales are everywhere. You need to be a good advertiser to be in the furniture business or have plenty of capital to survive the ups and downs. These are different businesses. If you are looking to hire a sales Manager. You may go in the direction of Newspaper, Career Builder or Indeed. You are looking for a specialist with lots of experience.

Let's look at a scenario that you are the manager of a clinic. You help the doctor run her dentist office. Dr. Smiles has tasked you to help her find a new dental assistant. You handle payroll, and office duties, but fully understand what the dental assistant need to do. Your position is much like the furniture industry position we just used. You have experience and understand the responsibility of the position. Dr. Smiles will want a good candidate but has no problem teaching the right assistant. I am looking to advertise maybe with Indeed and possibly do a Craigslist ad. You may be wondering why I brought up craigslist. The reason is simple, most of the time a new trainee dental assistant will be younger. 20's instead 40's like the sales manger we looked at before. Lot's of younger people like Craigslist as it does a lot more than just advertise for positions. Craigslist does a wonderful job of helping you get inexpensive things. This is perfect for a college student. This position does not have insurance as it is part time, and a college student will probably be on his/her parents insurance plan. This is an introductory position. Understanding who you are looking for determines the media.

VP of Business Development. I am the Chief Operations Officer of my company, and I am looking to hire a Vice President to help train and run a location while I go open other offices in the financial sector. It is unlikely that you will find a VP on Craigslist, so let's not spend time thinking about something that is not likely to work. In this scenario, I am very limited on time. I need a leader who is highly qualified. I will not make a hiring mistake as this position, as the CEO is the person I answer to. I may look at taking out a newspaper ad or going with Indeed. Remember I am tight on time, but in a position of this magnitude hiring this person may be a full-time job for a period. I decide to contact a professional and use what is often referred to a headhunter. The official position is a recruiter. I utilize the power of a recruiter, because of the statement made previously. This may be a full-time job for a period. I can get a full-time person to do this and I still focus on my position. My boss will want a solid solution not excuses.

Creating the Advertisement

We have spent time going over scenarios, point of this is to help everyone understand a little bit about why you would do an advertisement, and why sometimes it just doesn't make sense. When creating a new advertisement a few questions must be asked. 1. What are you trying to accomplish? 2. Is the position full or part time? 3. What hours are you in need of? How will a new person fit into your company? Once you have answers to these questions you are ready to writ an ad.

There are many small things that you need to do in an ad. First thing is let them know if they are salaried or hourly. Is there insurance? What is expected of them needs to be stated in the ad. If I am looking for a salesman, then I let them know I am looking for a person who is consultative. At ABC we are about helping our customers. Example: If you have worked for a luxury brand car dealership or was a top closer in the Insurance business this position could be great for you. We know that car salesperson from 1995 is not doing it the same way anymore. If a saleswoman does their job most customers are led to a conclusion that this is right for them. Not sold but guided. When preparing the ad, be sure to give an example of a person that works for your company. This allows the candidate to self-evaluate. 75% of the work will be done in the ad and phone interview. Your time is valuable. Do not waste it.

What if I am a CEO and I am looking for the VP. The ad starts out stating the title needed, and gives that general idea, but I have had 100's of resumes come in from a person that had no qualifications to begin with. Example: At the VP of ABC you oversee the finances of our customers. We take and oath and believe it is our fiduciary responsibility to understand this first and foremost. Later in that same ad I may say: If you have consistently been in the top 10% of companies you worked for then we need to talk to you.

How about a cleaning company? It is easy for us to assume things because we do it every day and the routine has allowed us to forget some basics that we do every day. Like earlier when Lucy forgot to ask if her new assistant can handle adversity on the phone. It is easy to forget this, and we all make mistakes. Example: At ABC Cleaning we work with fortune 500 companies every day. It is a must that you are comfortable working in professional environments and can work unsupervised. While we are a small company, the right person will have opportunities to advance in the company. A self-starter will have a great chance to get the position. If you feel this is you, then we need your resume. Please send to *******@**** and include a paragraph with your qualifications and why you are the right person. Please include this in a word or PDF document. Please understand we will not reply unless our instructions are followed. What this did was make sure that the person can do what you ask. You need to be able to trust they will do their job. This gives you a solid start in their ability to listen.

Quality or Quantity

Here is a simple fact. If your goal is to get resumes, I can get that done with relative ease. As someone in charge of hiring the only goal is to get the right person. By asking all the correct questions like: What you are looking for this employee or contractor to do? Is pay a selling point or is it the company? Is the position a value position? What I mean by this is: why would an employee choose to take less money to work with your company? The answer is value. Does your company or position have this desire that they can measure in more detail than just a paycheck? This will help you funnel your thoughts towards an answer that does not change everything you do but allows you to do this in the flow of work. Needing an employee is important but settling is not a solution. You are looking for quality. Make simple statements in the advertisement are a must. Example: Please send an email describing your desire for the position in a Word or PDF document only. Include a paragraph about yourself and why you would be a good fit. What you just did is make sure they look up your company and must figure out why they are a good candidate. There is nothing worse than doing an interview and the person does not even know what you do. I literally will stop the interview and say this is not the right position for you. The best time to take care of a problem is before it happens. A little more work in the beginning will save a lot of time and headache later. When the resume comes in with no paragraph, then they are not an option. No need to call or say anything else with this person. They are not qualified as you asked them to be. This candidate has already shown you that they do not listen. The only answer is next. I really do not care what their resume says at that point.

When you start getting resumes, it is best to do a phone interview after confirming the time and date via email. If you did a good job with the email giving detailed directions, then you should never have a person ask who is this? The same rule applies here. If they are not prepared... Next. After this point you have now done the work to bring them in for the in-person interview. I am a firm believer that people act different on the phone as they do in person. Over a decade of hiring for many positions in multiple industries has allowed me to understand trends. For this reason, I like what I call a 2-part interview. I tell the person that when they come in for an interview that we do a 2-part interview process. Make them aware that they will be coming in 2 times to get hired. If a person thinks this is to cumbersome...next. When the interviewee comes in be sure to have a clipboard or tablet with an application ready for them. It shows them you are serious and respect their time. This will imply they do the same to you and promptly answer questions. Do not skip this step. If you have a front desk person make sure he/she is aware of this as well. When an interviewee comes, I fully expect they are aware of this importance of doing the interview. If you did your job on the phone there will be no issues. Let's go into this part in detail.

In my first sit down interview I am always dress top quality to meet my profession. If I am a CEO then attire is a suit. If own a cleaning company, them dress for the part, maybe uniforms with your company logo. The position company or job does not change your ability show complete professionalism, class, and integrity. Remember all business start out small. This is commonly known as a micro-business. There is no need to act differently than the position you are expecting. You are the same person in the interview as you are after hiring. Not getting off topic too much here. Back to the sit-down interview. In my first interview I will have already covered many things on the phone as previously discussed. This person already knows you are serious about filling the position. I like to ask 3 questions to every candidate. Every part of the interview is calculated to see what pro's and con's your interviewee has. If shortcuts are your thing, then hiring will be difficult for you. Expect high turnover. I am very aware that many people are rolling their eyes right now. Please remember, I have hired top management that has almost taken companies under because of shortcuts. Should hiring be different?

Steve Jobs built Apple into a mega empire and then after a power struggle was forced out by the board run by then CEO John Scully. In 1997 Bill Gates stepped in and saved Apple form the brink of bankruptcy. Steve Jobs was brought back in the mix and the rest is history. Apple at one time was the single most valuable company in the world. Apple is now worth more than Microsoft - go figure. So yes, hiring and finding talent is critical, knowing what to do with the talent is just as important as illustrated with Bill Gates and Steve Jobs. A leader can turn a company into a mega empire. A poor leader never had a chance. This starts with hiring and finding the right people to work with. If you don't have a plan, then you are gambling. If you understand the stock market then you are investing, but if you listen to people without proving the theory, then you are just guessing. Why is it that multiple billionaires have made more than one company a billion-dollar company? They have a model and it works. See Warren Buffet, Richard Branson, Elon Musk and so on.

Question 1a. What is your biggest strength? 1b. What is a weakness that we can help you with? This immediately catches them off guard and makes them think about your company as unique. They also must look at weakness(s) they may have. It is not something that gets asked much, so the advantage here is that you get to see how they respond off key. 2. I like to say to each interviewee: success is my duty and obligation to my staff and (customers, clients, patients etc.) What will you do to help make this come true when I hire you? Let them know you are thinking about hiring them by assuming they are the person. Notice they are answering this question thinking they are a top candidate. I am looking for reactions here, do not turn this into a formality making the candidate relax. 3. When can I start calling your references? I want the candidate on front of me to know I mean business. The entire process is made to find the right person. I keep the interview to a max of 20 minutes and, I may even mention it is 15 to 20 minutes on the phone beforehand.

Let's recap. We have run a well-prepared advertisement, did a phone interview (note: everybody gets the same phone interview) and finally did interview part one. On interview part two we want this to be different. Let's call it the mobile interview. When they come in just as before. They must know that you expected them. I have their resume and application on a clipboard. If I have a front desk person, they are aware of the interview and says congratulations. You made it to the 2nd interview. Would you like any coffee or water? If no front desk person, same concept it will just be done by you. Then have them wait for 5 to 10 minutes. When the interview starts, I get up and say: Congratulations you are one of a few final candidates I am serious about bringing aboard. We will now take them around and meet staff members or show them the highlights of what we do. This may include showing them the space they will work in like a nice window or executive chair; of the equipment they will be using and what size they wear for the embroidering of their polo shirt. The whole interview is done moving around to learn about posture and how they act meeting new people unexpectedly. We have done a lot of work to get to this point. Its' time to be sure and go over questions that may be lingering. Later, this will allow you to ask others what they saw. More eyes and different views can be great feedback. This first interview was about them understanding what you do, and the 2nd interview is about what they will be doing on a day to day basis. Let them know what is expected, and what will be done starting with day 1. As a hiring manager you must explain the expectations. It amazes me how many times people start on the first day with no idea. If you do this part in the interview, the new staff member will come in and understand the task day one, two and so on.

I want to get a quality person who fits what I am looking for. After three ways of interviewing you will have a great idea. Remember question #2 in the first interview. This was stated as hiring an employee is in many cases their livelihood. They are going to be spending lots of time with you or your staff. If you did part 2 correctly, they would know where to sit, or where to get started each day. This makes a new job must less awkward day one and makes them feel like a team member not just the newbie. This will make them feel like you are already including them in your staff. If all has handles properly, then the interview should be a fulfilling experience. You are different, so be different.

We have spent time going over scenarios, point of this is to help everyone involved understand a little bit about more about why you would do an advertisement, and why sometimes it just doesn't make sense. Every business is different, even though some industries are the same. Don't follow the industry standard but tread your own path forward. I didn't go into some simple nuances that people do like voice inflections or allowing your own personal leadership style to show. Utilizing these are very important to the overall success of your business, so please do the same in the interview process. In the book Zero to One by Peter Thiel "Look around. If you don't see any salespeople, you're the salesperson" This applies in many businesses. It is the same in the interview process. Salespeople do a good job of preparing their sales pitch. Master salespersons do such a great job that most people don't even know they are being sold. Peter Thiel talks about the 10X Rule. He doesn't discuss it the same way that Grant Cardone does, but both wildly successful businessmen believe that if you are 10 times better than your competition that you will have exponential success. This can turn into 20 or 30 times better as a result.

This may be a hard concept to swallow, but let's turn to sports for a minute. Every sports team is willing to go all in on a once in a lifetime talent like Lebron James in Basketball, or a world class pitcher in baseball. The reason is that this small improvement can mean a team winning for a decade or missing out and being mediocre. Hiring the best for a manager that will be the face of a location is really that important. Starbucks makes it a huge point to get hiring right, because each location must be held to the standard of the company. People will take less money to be a manager at Starbucks, knowing the job can be a steppingstone into a larger role later. Starbucks does not aim to hold people back but embraces the power of being a steppingstone. I have hired employees thinking that this could be the best hire I have ever made just to find out that he/she was not at all the person I was hiring. Like investing, even though you did a great job of vetting and understanding your stock, you still can get it wrong or be pleasantly surprised. A rule I have adapted is the late rule. If a person wants the job, they will be on time. If they are late to begin with, then you are starting a relationship with an excuse. The truth is much easier to start with. Here is the great thing about doing a 2-part interview. If you believe that 5 minutes late to the first interview was reasonable, then in part 2 you will not allow it to happen, and you can say we have your one late time out of the way. This allows for a fresh start and allows you the hiring manager to set the tone for what is expected in the future.

Examples of advertisements I would run in order to find candidates are below.

*** Medical Technician --- FULL TIME POSITION $18 Per Hour ***

($18 per Hour) All Daytime Hours working with a Licensed Medical Doctor

Full Time medical professional needed for unique specialty medical clinic We help Men and Women with Weight Loss. Please understand we work with lots of geriatric patients. This is a great position for a Medical Assistant, EMT, Paramedic and/or Nurse. You will work side by side with a licensed MD. Must be 100% dependable, have a positive personality, good work habits including, but not limited to enthusiasm and desire. We want our staff and patients to be comfortable with the work environment. Daytime Hours, no evenings, or weekends. Email resume in PDF or Word format and a brief note about why you would be a good fit for the position. We promote from within.

Beautiful medical building in (your city). Great staff to work with. Please note there will be a raise to $18.50 per hour after successful 3 months from start date. Important to be flexible. Thank You Management!

*** APPOINTMENT & CARE PROFESSIONAL --- Medical Office ***

Incoming calls and call backs (40K first year can earn $50K or more)

FULL-TIME telephone care professional needed for unique specialty medical clinic, take inbound calls from advertising we do in many media's, follow script and book appointments. High quality advertising done in house. You ABSOLUTELY MUST have at least (5) years' experience working on the telephone or inbound sales to be considered, be 100% dependable, have a positive personality, good work habits are a must. Due to the unique nature of our medical practice we request well-groomed applicants, thank you for understanding. Daytime Hours, no evenings, or weekends. $18 per hour plus patient care bonuses paid bi-weekly. Email resume with a brief note about yourself, and why you would be a good fit. Please send in Word or PDF document only. Beautiful medical building. Great staff to work with and we promote from within. Our website is ********@****.com please check out our state of the art website :)

***Dog Groomer Needed for ABC Dog Lovers --- $12 Hourly Part Time ***

PART TIME POSITION AFTERNOONS AND SATURDAY'S, we are looking for a groomer to fill the position of evening after school and Saturdays. This position is perfect if you aspire of working with animals or want an entry level position to look great on your resume. This is also great if you want to get a start with the veterinary. At ABC Dog Lovers we have helped others get their start in the vet industry. Please email us your resume in a Word or PDF document only to ********@***.com We hope the position will help raise the roof roof.

Now let's go to the top-level executive. We are looking to hire a CEO. This is a different style advertisement, this is a good choice for LinkedIn, Indeed, The Ladders, and Recruiters

Chief Executive Officer – CEO Needed for ABC Mon Company - Salary DOQ

Our CEO is responsible for providing strategic, financial and operational leadership for the company and will closely coordinate and work with the Board of Directors and senior leadership team.

Primary Responsibilities

1. Plan, develop, implement and direct the organization's operational and fiscal function and performance.
2. Act as a strategic partner by developing and implementing the company's plans and programs.

3. Analyze and make recommendation on the impact of long-range growth initiatives, planning, and introduction of new strategies and regulatory actions.
4. Develop credibility and authority for the finance leadership team by providing accurate analysis of budgets, reports and financial trends and operational procedures in order to assist the BOD and senior executive team.
5. Create, improve, implement and enforce policies and procedures of the organization that will improve operational and financial effectiveness of the company.
6. Communicate effectively and establish credibility throughout the organization and with the Board of Directors as an effective developer of solutions to business challenges.
7. Provide expert financial guidance and advice to others within executive leadership.
8. Improve the planning and budgeting process on a continual basis by educating departments and key members of corporate leadership.
9. Provide strategic input and leadership on decision making issues affecting the organization; specifically relating to the evaluation of potential mergers, acquisitions or partnerships.
10. Optimize the handling of banking relationships and work closely with CFO to foster and grow strategic financial partnerships.
11. Work with finance team to develop a solid cash flow projection and reporting mechanism, which includes setting a minimum cash threshold to meet operating needs.
12. Act as a strategic advisor and consultant offering expert advice on contracts, negotiations or business

deals that the corporation may consider later entering into.
13. Evaluate company's financial, operational, and sales and marketing structures to plan for continual improvements and a continual increase of operating efficiencies.
14. Mentor and interact with members of staff at all levels to foster growth and encourage development among senior executive team and all members of staff.

Important Leadership Traits:

1. Strong leadership ability.
2. Strategic mindset.
3. Professional business acumen.
4. Outstanding problem-solving skills.
5. Excellent ability to lead and manage
6. Continually drive effective results.
7. Communicate effectively at all levels.

Requirements and Preferred Qualifications:

1. Bachelor's degree in business or related, MBA from top school preferred
2. 5-10 years of industry experience.
3. Ability to train, develop and manage large executive teams
4. Executive Presence and ability maintain calm demeanor in high stress environments

I hope your business the very best. There are many more tips, and secrets, but I gave you an honest way to get a hiring off the ground. Just go to http://businessbuildersconsulting.com if

you some guidance from one of my excellent colleagues and business partners. I leave you with this quote:

"In This Time of Constant Information Ignorance is a Choice"

 Justin Webster